THE HALF

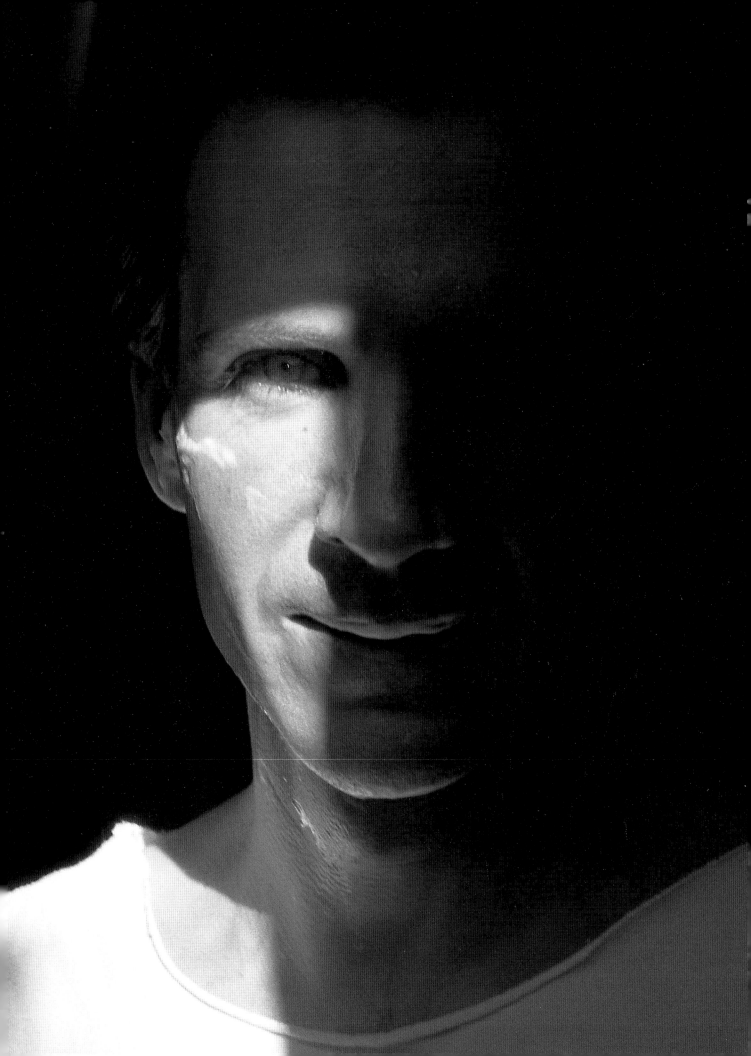

The Half

Photographs of Actors Preparing for the Stage

Simon Annand

ff

faber and faber

Frontis: **Ralph Fiennes**
Coriolanus & Richard II by William Shakespeare
Almeida Theatre at Gainsborough Studios, 2000
Ralph Fiennes lit by the sun, shaving, in the
temporary Shoreditch dressing rooms. He was
playing both leads, in rep

First published in 2008
by Faber and Faber Limited
3 Queen Square, London WC1N 3AU

Designed and typeset by Patrick Eley
Picture editing by Simon Annand, Barney Wan
& Caroline Fellus
Printed in Germany by Appl Druck, Wemding

A CIP record for this book
is available from the British Library

ISBN 978–0–571–23772–2

10 9 8 7 6 5 4 3 2 1

For Caroline
and
The Old Man of Oakhurst

FOREWORD
Simon Annand

The image to the left is the exact moment when photography entered my life, even though the picture was taken by a complete stranger.

A holiday-maker was passing by and I gave him my father's camera to mark a moment when my family was fully happy. It was important to me that somehow this rare event was recorded. My brother, my hero, was still talking to me, my adopted sister felt at ease, my mother, standing just behind me, was surprised by my daring, and my father was proud that the foreign holiday, which he had paid for at great expense, was a success. It was high summer, at the seaside, 1961, and my world felt complete.

Twenty-two years later I was working in the bar at the Lyric Theatre, Hammersmith, while Griff Rhys-Jones was giving his wonderful performance in *Charley's Aunt*. His perfect comic timing and high energy kept the joyous waves of laughter rolling in, night after night. The funniest moment of all came when he poured tea into his beloved father's top hat (*far left*) and, during my often dull shift pulling pints, I used to secretly steal into the wings and breathe in the excitement coming over the footlights from the auditorium. It gave me such pleasure to witness Griff's hold over his audience that I decided to take a photograph, without consent, from the lighting fly-tower. This was my first ever theatre production photograph.

Another high point in Griff's performance was the entrance he made through a window into Lord Fancourt Babberley's apartments. I asked Griff if I could photograph him behind the scenery (*centre*), just before he made this entrance, when he summoned up the jolly bravura of the character.

Access to this process, the construction of a performance, was strangely thrilling, so once again I asked Griff if I could photograph him, this time one step removed from the stage, in the dressing room (*bottom*). There I found him to be reflective, quiet, and almost melancholy.

The difference in energy fascinated me and these three images became the beginning of a book which set out to explore an actor's journey from the dressing room to the stage. Each photograph in *The Half* has been hand-picked by me for many different reasons: personal, historical, the performances, the rooms themselves, and so on. The selection of photographs is not intended to be comprehensive in any way.

To uncover this secret narrative I have received invaluable assistance from numerous people – stage managers, company managers, dressers, stage-doorkeepers, agents, friends and family – to whom I owe my deepest gratitude.

A collection of photographic prints does not necessarily make a book; this has ultimately been achieved through the guidance of Dinah Wood, my editor, whose wisdom and humour is an example to all who have the good fortune to work with her. I am grateful to everyone involved with the book at Faber, especially Stephen Page.

Thank you Michael Kustow for your inspiration.

These photographs show a world that is not normally seen, and I am forever indebted to all the actors who have allowed me privileged access to share their private space before they go on stage to face an audience.

viii   **Robert Lepage**
The Andersen Project
Barbican, 2006
Written, directed & performed
by Robert Lepage

INTRODUCTION
Michael Kustow

Their life is a voluntary dream; a studied madness… Today kings, tomorrow beggars… They show us all that we are, all that we wish to be, and all that we dread to be.

William Hazlitt
On Actors & the Art of Acting, 1813

Twenty-five years ago, Simon Annand began to photograph actors in and around their dressing rooms as they prepared for the evening's performance. This book contains his own selection of images, the variety and intimacy of which capture the many different ways that actors choose to spend the sacrosanct half-hour before curtain-up.

As every actor will tell you, 'the half' is not even a round thirty minutes, more like thirty-five, to ensure every actor is fully ready and in place five minutes before the play begins. Like 'flies', 'flats', 'trap', 'tread', 'apron', 'stalls' and 'gods', the half has become part of theatre lingo; and an iron law for every actor. Stage-doorkeepers usher through panicky latecomers, stage managers acquire the authority of cricket umpires. If you haven't signed in by the half, you'd better have a very good reason.

The half is a tense and vulnerable time; if acting were religion, you might call the half the ascent towards a part. Whatever has occurred during the day must be channelled or contained in readiness for the work that lies ahead. This journey, from person to persona, is a private one; it is rare for a photographer to be admitted. Certainly none has travelled so far with the actors – and not with the empathy, knowledge and conviction – as Simon Annand. These are pre-performance, pre-entrance photographs, arising from a contract between photographer and subject. The rigour of the half is reflected in the images' underlying gravity, even when the actors are apparently letting off steam, playing cards or the guitar, or sleeping. Here you will find a matchless anthology – almost an anthropological survey – of actors' external warm-ups and inner reflections, their quietness and their exuberance, their self-communion, self-scrutiny and self-abandon.

There are photographs of faces which, over years of performances, have become impregnated by what they do. Actors are like the dyer in Shakespeare's sonnet, his hand indelibly stained: 'my nature is subdued / To what it works in'. You can see that here on the faces of the most experienced: Vanessa Redgrave, Colin Blakely, Michael Gambon, Frances de la Tour, Anthony Hopkins, Ian McKellen. They are creatures possessed, inhabited by the succession of strangers to whom they have given habitation, an accumulation of lodgers who have left marks, etched features. Annand has captured these afterlives, these facial and bodily memories.

Equally enticing are images of the new generation: Daniel Radcliffe preparing for *Equus*, Ruth Wilson making her first appearance at the National, Laurence Fox in *Treats*, Ben Whishaw about to play Hamlet at the Old Vic, Jodie Whittaker at the Almeida. And then there are those actors who, now famous, were photographed by Simon Annand before they

Matthew Rhys
The Graduate by Terry Johnson, based on
the novel by Charles Webb and the screenplay
by Calder Willingham & Buck Henry
Gielgud Theatre, 2000

became household names, such as Colin Firth, Daniel Day Lewis, Kenneth Branagh, Tim Roth, Gary Oldman.

But these photographs document not only the actors but also their working conditions, and there is another major player: the dressing room itself. A bare space of work-top, a gown-rail, mirror, lights and, more often than not, whitewashed brick walls and a communal lavatory in the corridor. Annand, who also has extensive experience as a production photographer, is the first to make the dressing room the hub of his exploration of theatre.

The psychoanalyst Melanie Klein coined the phrase 'transitional object' to describe the dolls, toys, fetish objects that a child chooses in the journey from dependency on its mother's breast to free-standing autonomy. Actors likewise turn the transitional space of an empty dressing room into their transitory home, hung with good-luck cards, favourite images and potent charms. Juliet Stevenson creates her own gallery on the bare walls; Christopher Eccleston is overlooked by a poster of Strindberg, in whose play *Miss Julie* he is appearing. From the apparent opulence of Judi Dench's dressing room at the Haymarket, in which Gielgud spent occasional nights during the war, to the King's Head, Islington, possibly the least spacious of them all, where men and women change together beneath a leaking roof, the dressing room is a place of passage between the regime of real life and the liberty of an invented one.

The drama in these photographs is the drama of theatre-workers under pressure, which is why they are so different from posed portraits or production stills. The images have a rare candour and integrity; their ethos is as frank as that of live theatre itself. There is no sorcery, only the rough magic of actors preparing to make 'make believe'. These photographs evoke the care – and the carefreeness – the rigour and the erotic magnetism that feed each performance. They do so subtly and indirectly, by scrupulous and steady observation of actors in the dressing room, the room of change, getting ready for the night's work.

The Half is many things: a cross-section of British theatre over twenty-five years, a manual of ways to prepare to perform, a sequence of arresting, touching, hilarious and often weirdly surreal images. Above all, these photographs are the work of a heart and a sensibility in love with live theatre.

THE HALF

2 **Lia Williams**
Absurd Person Singular by Alan Ayckbourn
Garrick Theatre, 2008

Matt Smith
Swimming with Sharks by Michael Lesslie,
based on the film by George Huang
Vaudeville Theatre, 2007

Orlando Bloom
In Celebration by David Storey
Duke of York's Theatre, 2007

6   **Martin Sheen**
     The Normal Heart by Larry Kramer
     Royal Court Theatre, 1986
     A production that raised early
     awareness about AIDS

8   **Billie Whitelaw**
Rockaby written & directed by Samuel Beckett
Riverside Studios, 1989

10   Men's dressing room:
      Richard Hollis, Graham Seed,
      Christopher Terry, Dudley Hinton
      & Edward Bennett

      Women's dressing room:
      Julie Teal, Charity Reindorp,
      Daisy Ashford, Miriam Hughes
      & Lynn Farleigh

      The Skin Game by John Galsworthy
      Orange Tree Theatre, 2007
      Fringe-theatre dressing rooms
      – committed actors working in
      cramped conditions

12 **Jos Vantyler & Lucie Dobbing**
Charley's Aunt by Brandon Thomas
New Wimbledon Theatre, 2007

Rachael Stirling
Theatre of Blood by Lee Simpson
& Phelim McDermott
National Theatre, 2005

Ben Whishaw
Hamlet by William Shakespeare
Old Vic Theatre, 2004
Twenty-three years old and
preparing to play the lead

Stephen Boxer
Antarctica by David Young
Savoy Theatre, 2001

16 **Andrea Riseborough**
The Pain and the Itch by Bruce Norris
Royal Court Theatre, 2007

Jude Law
'Tis Pity She's a Whore by John Ford
Young Vic Theatre, 1999

Cillian Murphy
Love Song by John Kolvenbach
New Ambassadors Theatre, 2006
Barely a cupboard, the smallest
dressing room in the book

Michael Hordern
You Never Can Tell by Bernard Shaw
Theatre Royal Haymarket, 1987

Daniel Radcliffe
Equus by Peter Shaffer
Gielgud Theatre, 2007

Robert Eddison
The Infernal Machine by Jean Cocteau
Lyric Theatre, Hammersmith, 1986
A contemporary of John Gielgud

22   **Jeremy Irons**
The Rover by Aphra Behn
Swan Theatre, Stratford-upon-Avon, 1986

Embers by Christopher Hampton,
based on the novel by Sándor Márai
Duke of York's Theatre, 2006

Jonathan Cecil
The Hypochondriac by Molière,
in a translation by Alan Drury
Lyric Theatre, Hammersmith, 1987

Miriam Karlin
Lavochkin – 5 by Alexie Shipenko,
in a translation by Iain Heggie & Irina Brown
Tron Theatre, Glasgow, 1997

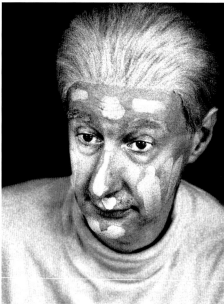

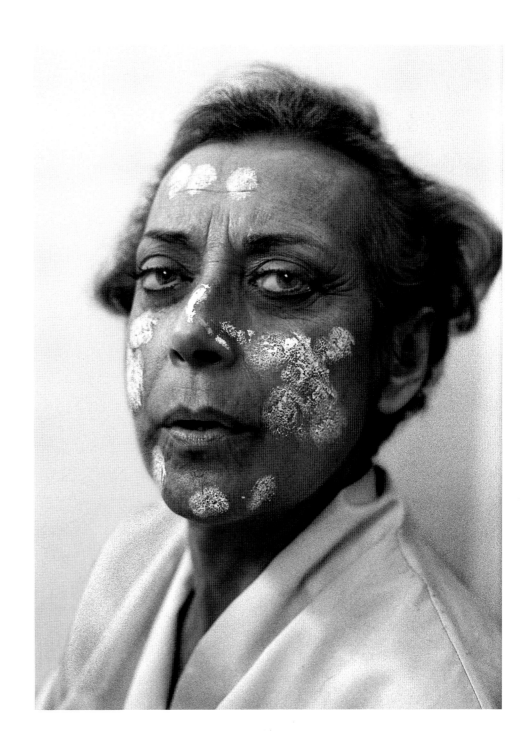

28   **Francesca Annis**
      Three Sisters by Anton Chekhov,
      in a translation by Michael Frayn
      Albery Theatre, 1987

      Frank Finlay
      Mutiny! by Richard Crane
      Piccadilly Theatre, 1985

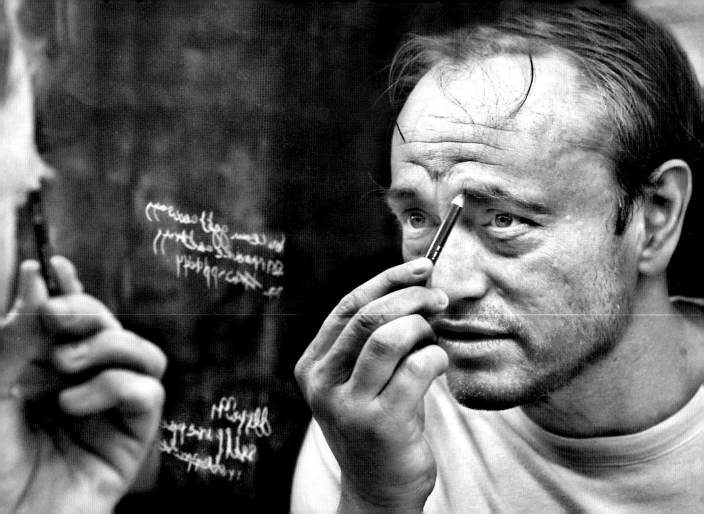

Colin Firth
The Lonely Road by Arthur Schnitzler,
in a translation by Ronald Adam &
Christopher Fettes
Old Vic Theatre, 1985

David Tennant
The Rivals by Richard Brinsley Sheridan
Barbican Theatre, 2000

Laurence Fox
Treats by Christopher Hampton
Garrick Theatre, 2007

James Jagger
Lone Star & *Private Wars* by James McLure
King's Head Theatre, 2007

Mary Rose & Carey Mulligan
The Seagull by Anton Chekhov,
in a version by Christopher Hampton
Royal Court Theatre, 2007

Dan Stevens
Hay Fever by Noël Coward
Theatre Royal Haymarket, 2006
Leaping downstairs towards the stage,
past Judi Dench's dressing room

38 **Catherine Tate**
The Exonerated by Jessica Blank & Eric Jensen
Riverside Studios, 2006
Not a cigarette, but a lollypop

Jane Bertish
A Family Affair by Alexander Ostrovsky,
in a translation by Nick Dear
Arcola Theatre, 2006

Roger Delves-Broughton & Tim Treslove
Dick Whittington by Nick Mowat
Mercury Theatre, Colchester, 2002

Simon Callow
The Relapse by Sir John Vanbrugh
Lyric Theatre, Hammersmith, 1983
The photographer appeared as a servant
in this production, and carried Simon Callow
off stage every night in a sedan chair

Timothy Walker
La Bête by David Hirson
Lyric Theatre, Hammersmith, 1992

42 **Rhys Ifans**
Accidental Death of an Anarchist
by Dario Fo
Donmar Warehouse, 2003

Penelope Dimond
Much Ado about Nothing
by William Shakespeare
Shakespeare's Globe Theatre, 2004

Stephen Dillane
Uncle Vanya by Anton Chekhov,
in a version by David Lan
Young Vic Theatre, 1998

James Fleet
Three Sisters by Anton Chekhov,
in a version by Christopher Hampton
Playhouse Theatre, 2003

44 **Elizabeth McGovern**
    Hurly Burly by David Rabe
    Old Vic Theatre, 1997

    Ruth Wilson
    Philistines by Maxim Gorky,
    in a version by Andrew Upton
    National Theatre, 2007

Saffron Burrows
Some Girls by Neil LaBute
Gielgud Theatre, 2005

Maureen Lipman
The Vagina Monologues
by Eve Ensler
Arts Theatre, 2001

Adrian Scarborough
Once in a Lifetime by Moss Hart
& George S. Kaufman
National Theatre, 2006

Elena Rogers
Evita by Tim Rice & Andrew Lloyd Webber
Adelphi Theatre, 2006

Juliette Lewis
Fool for Love by Sam Shepard
Apollo Theatre, 2006

David Schwimmer
Some Girls by Neil LaBute
Gielgud Theatre, 2005
The day after the London bombings

Iain Glen
A Streetcar Named Desire
by Tennessee Williams
National Theatre, 2002

54 **Harish Patel**
Rafta, Rafta… by Ayub Khan-Din,
based on *All in Good Time* by Bill Naughton
National Theatre, 2007

Greg Hicks
Angels in America by Tony Kushner
Lyric Theatre, Hammersmith, 2007

Dorothy Tutin
A Kind of Alaska by Harold Pinter
Duchess Theatre, 1984

Aisling O'Sullivan
Miss Julie by August Strindberg,
in a version by Frank McGuinness
Theatre Royal Haymarket, 2000

Anthony Quayle
The Clandestine Marriage by George Colman the
Elder and David Garrick
Albery Theatre, 1984

Donald Sinden
The Scarlet Pimpernel by Emmuska Orczy
Her Majesty's Theatre, 1985

David Suchet
Man and Boy by Terence Rattigan
Duchess Theatre, 2005

Irène Jacob
Madame Melville by Richard Nelson
Vaudeville Theatre, 2000

Joanna Lumley
Blithe Spirit by Noël Coward
Vaudeville Theatre, 1986

Susan Hampshire
Relative Values by Alan Ayckbourn
Vaudeville Theatre, 1993

Kenneth Cranham
Gaslight by Patrick Hamilton
Old Vic Theatre, 2007

Alex Jennings
Too Clever by Half by Alexander Ostrovsky,
adapted by Rodney Ackland
Old Vic Theatre, 1988

Daniel Day Lewis
The Futurists by Dusty Hughes
National Theatre, 1986

68   **Joan Plowright**
The Way of the World by William Congreve
Theatre Royal Haymarket, 1984

Max von Sydow
The Tempest by William Shakespeare
Old Vic Theatre, 1988

Siân Phillips
Marlene by Pam Gems
Lyric Theatre, Shaftesbury Avenue, 1997

Julia Stiles
Oleanna by David Mamet
Garrick Theatre, 2004

Charlotte Rampling
The False Servant by Pierre Marivaux,
in a version by Martin Crimp
National Theatre, 2004

Christopher Eccleston
Maxine Peake
Aisling O'Sullivan
Miss Julie by August Strindberg,
in a version by Frank McGuinness
Theatre Royal Haymarket, 2000

Glenda Jackson
The House of Bernarda Alba by Federico García Lorca,
in a translation by Robert David MacDonald
Lyric Theatre, Hammersmith, 1986

Patience Collier
Lent by Michael Wilcox
Lyric Theatre, Hammersmith, 1983

Greta Scacchi
Airbase by Malcolm McKay
Arts Theatre, 1984

Miranda Richardson
A Lie of the Mind by Sam Shepard
Royal Court Theatre, 1987

Jennifer Ehle
The Real Thing by Tom Stoppard
Albery Theatre, 2000
On a hot summer's night in an
airless dressing room

Alan Bates
Yonadab by Peter Shaffer
National Theatre, 1986
Reflecting on his blue make-up

Jane Birkin
Women of Troy by Euripides,
in a translation by Kenneth McLeish
National Theatre, 1995

Hayley Carmichael
Casanova by Carol Ann Duffy
Lyric Theatre, Hammersmith, 2007
Just before the final show

Kathryn Hunter
King Lear by William Shakespeare
Young Vic Theatre, 1997
In the title role

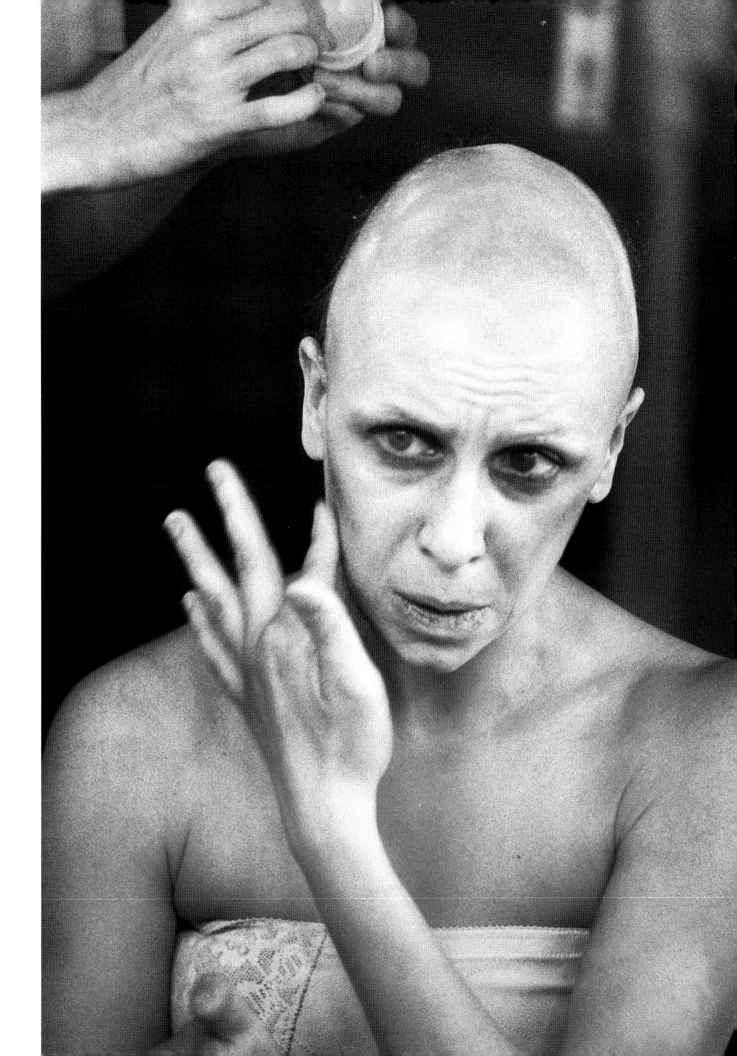

Helen McCrory
Twelfth Night by William Shakespeare
Donmar Warehouse, 2002

Sara Kestelman
Bussy d'Ambois by George Chapman
Old Vic Theatre, 1987

Mary Gifford with Jim Hooper
Salome by Oscar Wilde
Drama Centre, 2006

Sally Dexter
Macbeth by William Shakespeare
Queen's Theatre, 1999

Janet McTeer
A Doll's House by Henrik Ibsen,
in a version by Frank McGuinness
Playhouse Theatre, 1996

Eleanor Bron
The Miser by Molière,
in a translation by Jeremy Sams
National Theatre, 1991

Tilda Swinton
Mozart and Salieri by Aleksandr Pushkin
Almeida Theatre, 1989

Man to Man by Manfred Karge
Royal Court Theatre, 1987

Playing Mozart and, in *Man to Man*,
a woman who assumes her dead
husband's identity

94

Meera Syal
Rafta Rafta... by Ayub Khan-Din,
based on *All in Good Time* by Bill Naughton
National Theatre, 2007

Rosalind Knight
The Illusion by Pierre Corneille,
adapted by Ranjit Bolt
Old Vic Theatre, 1990

Angela de Castro
Slava's Snow Show by Slava Polunin
Old Vic Theatre, 1997

Dawn French
A Midsummer Night's Dream
by William Shakespeare
Albery Theatre, 2001

98

Marianne Jean-Baptiste
The Vagina Monologues by Eve Ensler
Arts Theatre, 2001

Jenny Jules
The Vagina Monologues by Eve Ensler
Arts Theatre, 2002

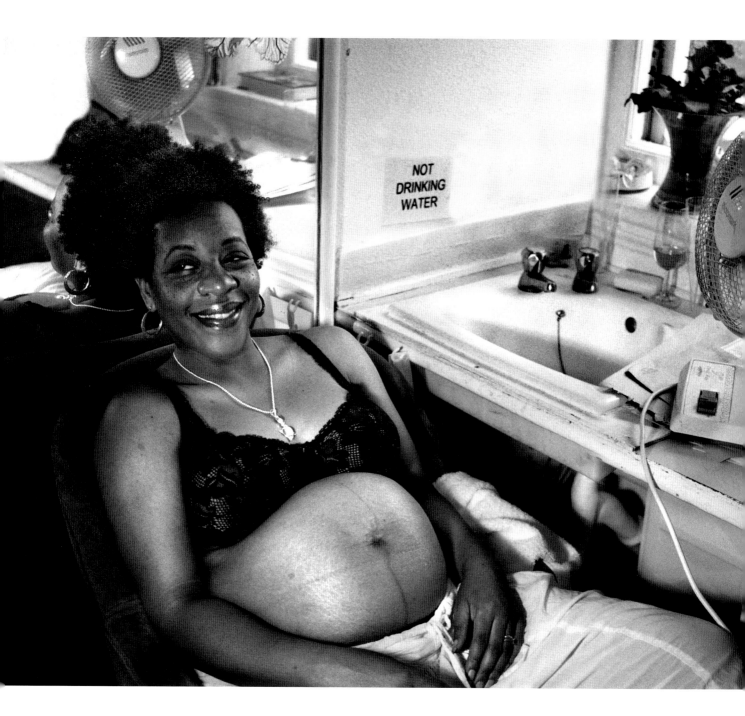

100

Liz Smith
Why Me? by Stanley Price
Strand Theatre, 1985
The day on which she received her BAFTA for Best
Supporting Actress in the film *A Private Function*

Patricia Hayes
The House of Bernarda Alba by Federico García Lorca,
in a translation by Robert David MacDonald
Lyric Theatre, Hammersmith, 1986

Mark Gatiss
All about My Mother by Samuel Adamson,
from the film by Pedro Almodóvar
Old Vic Theatre, 2007

Siobhan Hewlett
The Taming of the Shrew by William Shakespeare
Wilton's Music Hall, 2007

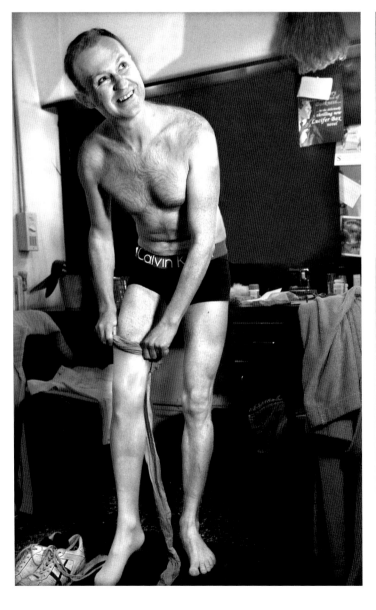
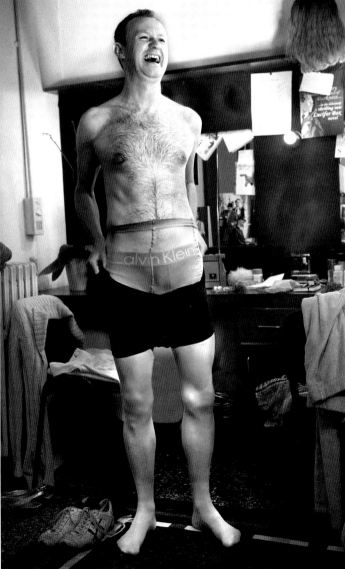

James Dreyfus
Cabaret by John Kander,
Fred Ebb & Joe Metseroff
Lyric Theatre,
Shaftesbury Avenue, 2006

Kristin Scott Thomas
Three Sisters by Anton Chekhov,
in a version by Christopher Hampton
Playhouse Theatre, 2003

The Seagull by Anton Chekhov,
in a version by Christopher Hampton
Royal Court Theatre, 2007

Antony Sher
Torch Song Trilogy by Harvey Fierstein
Albery Theatre, 1985

Ray Winstone
The Night Heron by Jez Butterworth
Royal Court Theatre, 2002

Eric Sykes
Dick Whittington
Theatre Royal, Bath, 1984

Ewan McGregor
Little Malcolm and His Struggle against the Eunuchs
by David Halliwell
Comedy Theatre, 1999

Ralph Fiennes
Coriolanus & Richard II by William Shakespeare
Almeida Theatre at Gainsborough Studios, 2000

Tim Pigott-Smith
Benefactors by Michael Frayn
Vaudeville Theatre, 1984

Ian McKellen
The Cut by Mark Ravenhill
Donmar Warehouse, 2006

Orlando Bloom
In Celebration by David Storey
Duke of York's Theatre, 2007

116

Ioan Gruffudd
The Play What I Wrote by Hamish McColl,
Sean Foley & Eddie Braben
Wyndham's Theatre, 2002

Rufus Sewell
Macbeth by William Shakespeare
Queen's Theatre, 1999

Jim Broadbent
A Flea in Her Ear by Georges Feydeau,
in a translation by John Mortimer
Old Vic Theatre, 1989

Oliver Ford Davis
Richard II by William Shakespeare
Almeida Theatre at Gainsborough Studios, 2000

Timothy West
Big in Brazil by Bamber Gascoigne
Old Vic Theatre, 1984

Bette Bourne
Theatre of Blood
by Lee Simpson & Phelim McDermott
National Theatre, 2005

Jenny Jules
Big White Fog by Theodore Ward
Almeida Theatre, 2007

Lesley Manville
Pillars of the Community by Henrik Ibsen,
in a version by Samuel Adamson
National Theatre, 2005

124 **Tony Armatrading**
Big White Fog by Theodore Ward
Almeida Theatre, 2007

Joe Renton
Henry IV Parts 1 & 2 by William Shakespeare
Barbican Theatre, 2000

**Lucian Msamati, Nick Fletcher, Adura Onashile,
Chipo Chung, Andrew Garfield & Babou Ceesay**
The Overwhelming by J. T. Rogers
National Theatre, 2006

Ian Dury
Apples by Ian Dury
Royal Court Theatre, 1989

Paul McGann
The Genius by Howard Brenton
Royal Court Theatre, 1983

Rory Kinnear
Philistines by Maxim Gorky,
in a version by Andrew Upton
National Theatre, 2007
On stage, practising the piano

Alison Steadman
Entertaining Mr Sloane
by Joe Orton
Arts Theatre, 2001
A blow-up lilo in the corridor
was the only space in which
to lie down

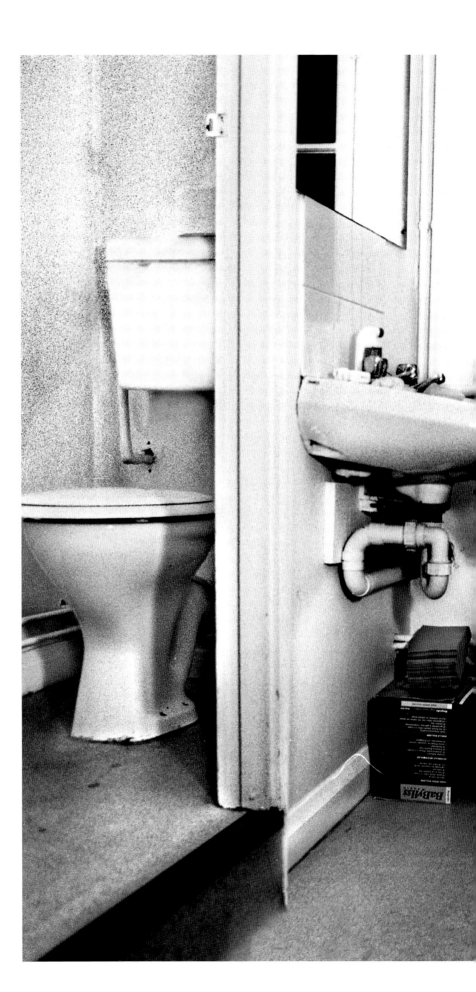

Rita Tushingham
The Vagina Monologues by Eve Ensler
Arts Theatre, 2001

Julie Walters
When I Was a Girl I Used to Scream and Shout
by Sharman Macdonald
Whitehall Theatre, 1986

140 **Ben Kingsley**
Othello by William Shakespeare
Barbican Theatre, 1985

Hugh Quarshie
Great White Hope by Howard Sackler
Tricycle Theatre, 1986

Holly Hunter
By the Bog of Cats by Marina Carr
Wyndham's Theatre, 2004
Taken at the final performance:
the black dress at the beginning,
and the white at the end

Patrick Stewart
Macbeth by William Shakespeare
Chichester Festival Theatre, 2007

Simon Russell Beale & Paul Jesson
Twelfth Night by William Shakespeare
Donmar Warehouse, 2002

Jonny Lee Miller
Festen by David Eldridge, based on the film and play
by Thomas Vinterberg, Morgens Rukov & Bo hr. Hansen
Lyric Theatre, Shaftesbury Avenue, 2004

Simon Scardifield
The Taming of the Shrew by William Shakespeare
Old Vic Theatre, 2007

Samuel West
The Exonerated by Jessica Blank & Eric Jensen
Riverside Studios, 2007

Alex Kingston
One Flew over the Cuckoo's Nest
by Ken Kesey, adapted by Dale Wasserman
Gielgud Theatre, 2004

Jerry Hall with George Costigan
The Graduate written & directed by Terry Johnson,
based on the novel by Charles Webb and the
screenplay by Calder Willingham & Buck Henry

Maiŕead McKinley
10 Rounds by Carlo Gébler
Tricycle Theatre, 2002

Imelda Staunton
Guys and Dolls by Frank Loesser & Abe Burrows
National Theatre, 1982

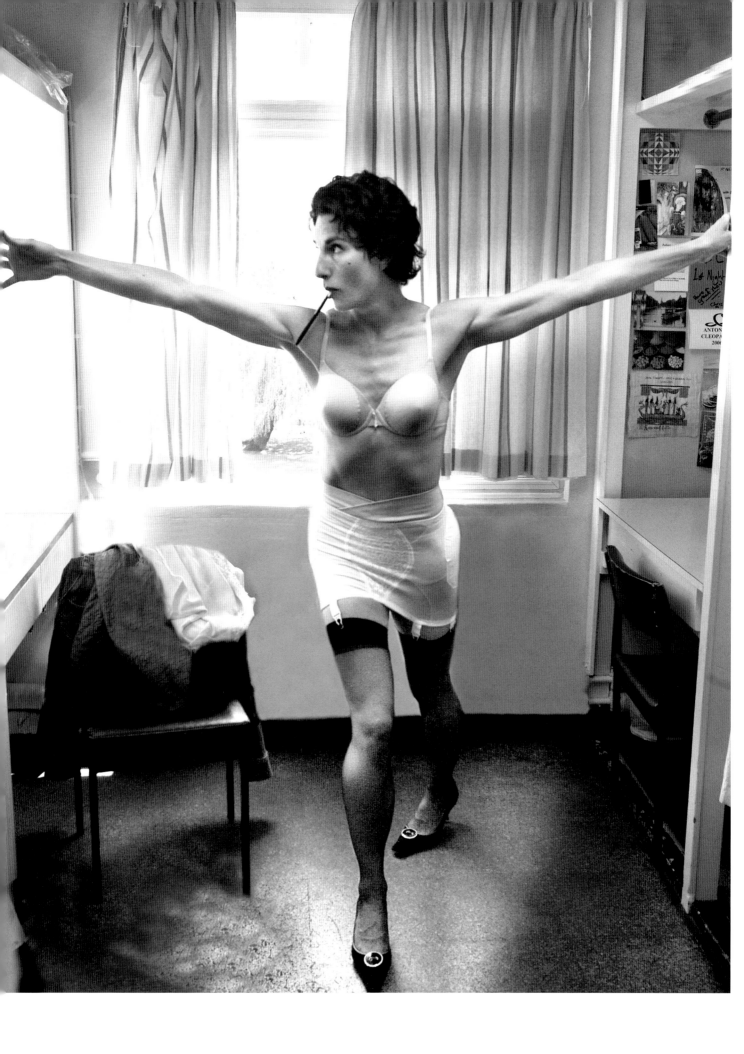

Tamsin Greig
Much Ado about Nothing by William Shakespeare
Swan Theatre, Stratford-upon-Avon, 2006
Trying on padded hips and bra to play Beatrice in
a Cuban version of the play

Hayley Atwell
The Man of Mode by George Etherege
National Theatre, 2007

Rosamund Pike
Gaslight by Patrick Hamilton
Old Vic Theatre, 2007

Jane Krakowski
Guys and Dolls by Frank Loesser & Abe Burrows
Piccadilly Theatre, 2005

Anne Marie Duff
Saint Joan by Bernard Shaw
National Theatre, 2007

Lindsay Duncan
That Face by Polly Stenham
Royal Court Theatre, 2007

160 **Janet Suzman**
Vassa by Maxim Gorky, adapted by Helena Kaut-Howson
Greenwich Theatre, 1985

Harriet Walter
The Royal Family by George S. Kaufman & Edna Ferber
Theatre Royal Haymarket, 2002

Romola Garai
Calico by Michael Hastings
Duke of York's Theatre, 2004
In the alley outside the stage door

Amita Dhiri
Whose Life Is It Anyway? by Brian Clark
Comedy Theatre, 2005
On the stage door's steps

164

Anna Madeley
Ladybird by Vassily Sigarev,
translated by Sasha Dugdale
Royal Court Theatre, 2004

Kelly Reilly
Piano/Forte written & directed
by Terry Johnson
Royal Court Theatre, 2006

Karl Johnson & Paul Ritter
The Night Heron by Jez Butterworth
Royal Court Theatre, 2002

166 **Eve Best**
'Tis Pity She's a Whore by John Ford
Young Vic Theatre, 1999

Alan Rickman
Private Lives by Noël Coward
Albery Theatre, 2001
Amused to be surrounded by signs
telling people what not to do

Michael Pennington
Crime and Punishment by Fyodor Dostoevsky,
adapted & directed by Yuri Lyubimov
Lyric Theatre, Hammersmith, 1983

Sweet William by Michael Pennington
Little Angel Theatre, 2007
Two photographs, twenty-five years apart

Joseph Fiennes & Leader Hawkins
Edward II by Christopher Marlowe
Crucible Theatre, Sheffield, 2001

Lee Ingleby
A Midsummer Night's Dream
by William Shakespeare
Albery Theatre, 2001

Roger Lloyd Pack & Johnny Hutch
A Flea in Her Ear by Georges Feydeau,
in a translation by John Mortimer
Old Vic Theatre, 1989

Gawn Grainger & Felicity Kendal
Amy's View by David Hare
Garrick Theatre, 2006

James Cromwell
Long Day's Journey into Night by Eugene O'Neill
Druid Theatre Company, Town Hall Theatre,
Galway, 2007

Kim Cattrall
Whose Life Is It Anyway? by Brian Clark
Comedy Theatre, 2005

Jemma Redgrave
A Midsummer Night's Dream by William Shakespeare
Albery Theatre, 2001

Corin Redgrave
Measure for Measure by William Shakespeare
Young Vic Theatre, 1987

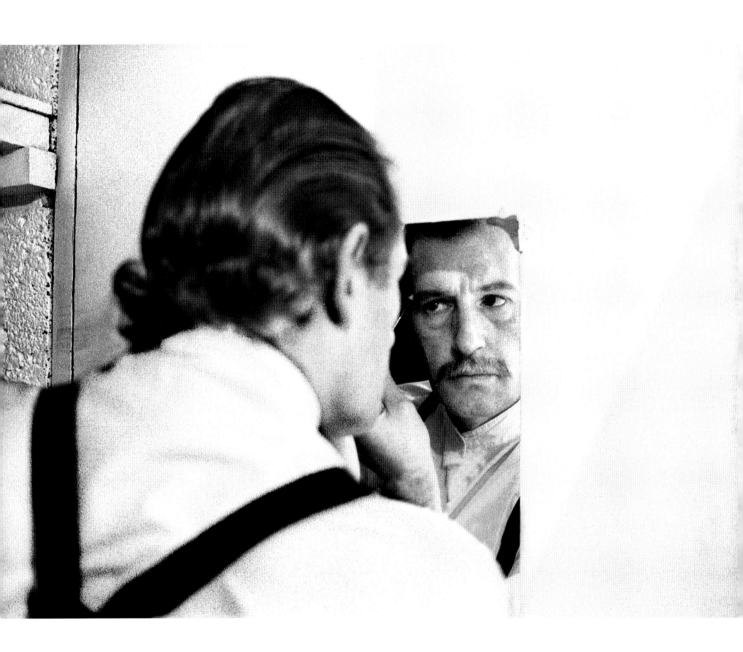

Eileen Atkins
There Came a Gypsy Riding by Frank McGuinness
Almeida Theatre, 2007
Picking up a piece of green jade given to her by
Alec Guinness. He bought it with his first week's
West End wages in 1934, and passed it on to her
after his final stage performance in 1989

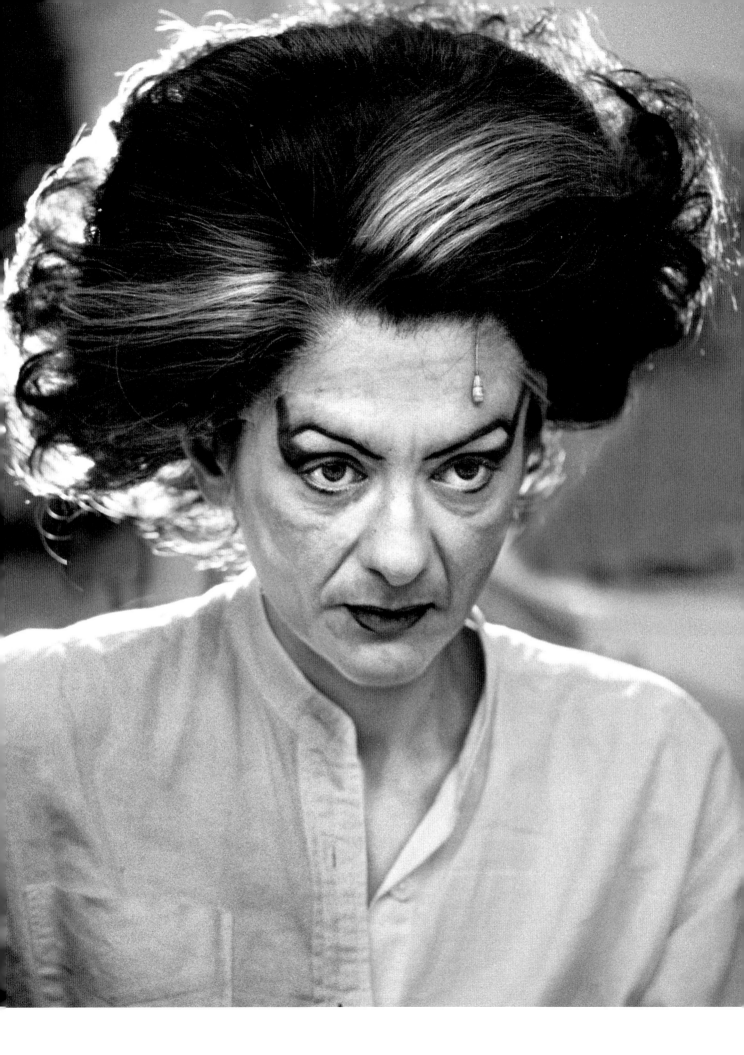

Shelley King
Bombay Dreams, music by A. R. Rahman,
lyrics by Don Black, book by Meera Syal
Apollo Victoria, 2002

Gillian Anderson
What the Night Is For by Michael Weller
Comedy Theatre, 2002

182 **Andy Serkis**
Mojo by Jez Butterworth
Royal Court Theatre, 1995

Peter Bowles
Joe and I by Laurie Slade
King's Head Theatre, 2005

Tom Hollander
Mojo by Jez Butterworth
Royal Court Theatre, 1995

Sylvestra Le Touzel
The Illusion by Pierre Corneille,
in a translation by Ranjit Bolt
Old Vic Theatre, 1990

Timothy Walker
A Flea in Her Ear by Georges Feydeau,
in a translation by John Mortimer
Old Vic Theatre, 1989

186　**Andrew Sachs**
Dick Whittington
Theatre Royal, Bath, 1984

Jane Horrocks
Sweet Panic
by Stephen Poliakoff
Duke of York's Theatre, 2004

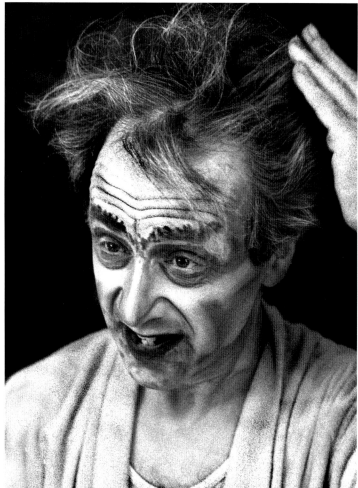

Marie Mullen
Long Day's Journey into Night by Eugene O'Neill
Druid Theatre Company, Town Hall Theatre,
Galway, 2007

Michelle Gomez
The Vagina Monologues by Eve Ensler
Arts Theatre, 2002

Janet Henfrey
Too Clever by Half by Alexander Ostrovsky,
adapted by Rodney Ackland
Old Vic Theatre, 1988

Frances de la Tour
Facades by William Humble
Lyric Theatre, Hammersmith, 1988

Spike Milligan
Babes in the Wood adapted by John Morley
Chichester Festival Theatre, 1985

Max Wall
Krapp's Last Tape by Samuel Beckett
Riverside Studios, 1989

Frances Barber
Camille by Alexandre Dumas, adapted by Neil Bartlett
Comedy Theatre, 1985

Diana Quick
Progress by Doug Lucie
Lyric Theatre, Hammersmith, 1986

198 **Fiona Shaw**
As You Like It by William Shakespeare
Old Vic Theatre, 1989

Marina Morgan
Remembrance of Things Past by Marcel Proust,
adapted by Harold Pinter & Di Trevis
National Theatre, 2000

Natasha Richardson
The Seagull by Anton Chekhov,
in a translation by Tania Alexander & Charles Sturridge
Lyric Theatre, Hammersmith, 1985

Joely Richardson
Beauty and the Beast by Louise Page
Old Vic Theatre, 1985

Rachel Kempson
Vanessa Redgrave
Ghosts by Henrik Ibsen,
translated by Peter Watts
Young Vic Theatre, 1986

Toby Stephens
The Royal Family by George S. Kaufman & Edna Ferber
Theatre Royal Haymarket, 2002
Toby Stephens, son of Maggie Smith, had requested a
room near the theatre's roof, to play his electric guitar
without disturbing the other actors. Like Judi Dench,
also in the cast and three floors below, he was filming
the James Bond film *Die Another Day*, during the day

Maggie Smith
Interpreters by Ronald Harwood
Queen's Theatre, 1986

Sorcha Cusack
The Five Wives of Maurice Pinder
by Matt Charman
National Theatre, 2007
Gesturing to actors across the
NT courtyard

Catherine Cusack
Brontë by Polly Teale
Lyric Theatre, Hammersmith, 2005

Sinéad Cusack
A Lie of the Mind by Sam Shepard
Donmar Warehouse, 2001

Emilia Fox
Richard II by William Shakespeare
Almeida Theatre at Gainsborough Studios, 2000

Edward Fox
You Never Can Tell by Bernard Shaw
Theatre Royal Haymarket, 1988
During the session, water was dripping
through the ceiling

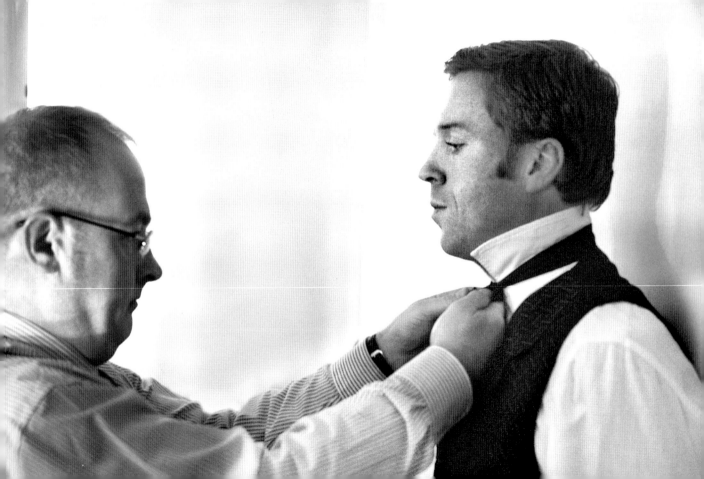

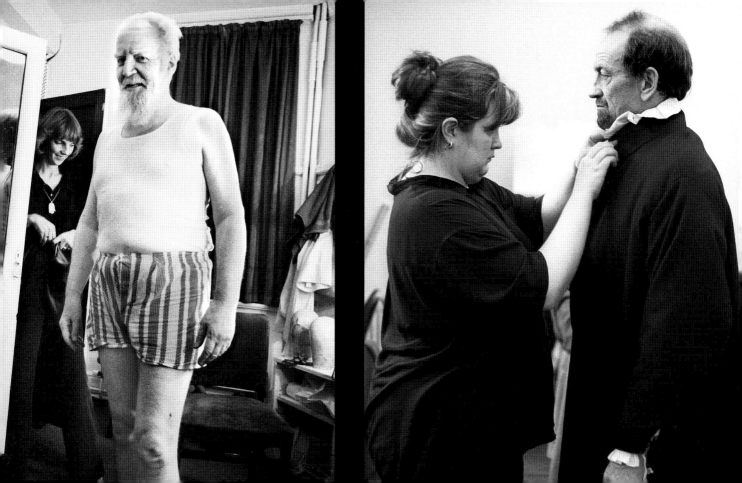

Clare Holman & Brid Brennan
10 Rounds by Carlo Gébler
Tricycle Theatre, 2002

Mackenzie Crook & Kristin Scott Thomas
The Seagull by Anton Chekhov,
in a version by Christopher Hampton
Royal Court Theatre, 2007

Joseph Fiennes
Edward II by Christopher Marlowe
Crucible Theatre, Sheffield, 2001

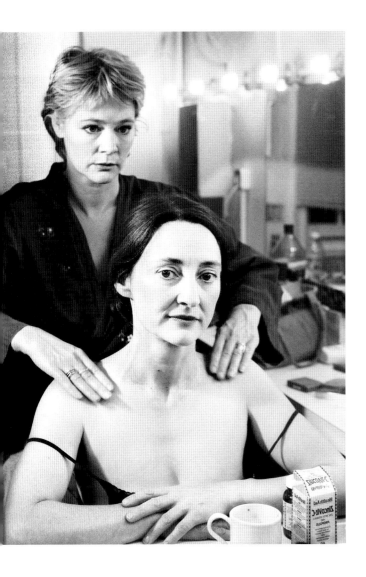

Rob Lowe
A Few Good Men by Aaron Sorkin
Theatre Royal Haymarket, 2005

Antony Sher
Torch Song Trilogy by Harvey Fierstein
Albery Theatre, 1985

Charity Reindorp
The Skin Game by John Galsworthy
Orange Tree Theatre, 2007

**Emma Gregory, Shuna Snow,
Christine Absalom & Miranda Floy**
The Duchess of Malfi by John Webster
Mercury Theatre, Colchester, 2000

Repairs and wardrobe: actors faring
for themselves

**Amanda Harris, Joyce Henderson
& Aicha Kossoko**
Macbeth by William Shakespeare
Battersea Arts Centre, 2000

Martin Sheen
The Normal Heart by Larry Kramer
Royal Court Theatre, 1986

Martin Henderson
Fool for Love by Sam Shepard
Apollo Theatre, 2006

Benedict Cumberbatch
Hedda Gabler by Henrik Ibsen,
in a version by Richard Eyre
Almeida Theatre, 2005

Checking props

Norman Beaton
Krapp's Last Tape by Samuel Beckett
Shaw Theatre, 1987
Spending time on stage before the audience arrives

Juliet Rylance
Bash by Neil LaBute
Trafalgar Studios, 2007
With reference material (photo by Richard Avedon)
to help her to find her character

Desmond Barrit
Jack and the Beanstalk by Desmond Barrit
Norwich Theatre Royal, 1996

David Oyelowo
Henry VI Part 3 by William Shakespeare
Swan Theatre, Stratford-upon-Avon, 2001
The first black actor to play one of
Shakespeare's kings for the RSC

Mark Rylance
Henry V by William Shakespeare
Shakespeare's Globe Theatre, 1997

Simon Russell Beale
Monty Python's *Spamalot*
Palace Theatre, 2007

Niamh Cusack
The Tutor by J. M. R. Lenz
Old Vic Theatre, 1987

Cyril Nri
The Tempest by William Shakespeare
Old Vic Theatre, 1988
The Old Vic basement. A photo of the
legendary impresario Lillian Baylis is
on the wall behind

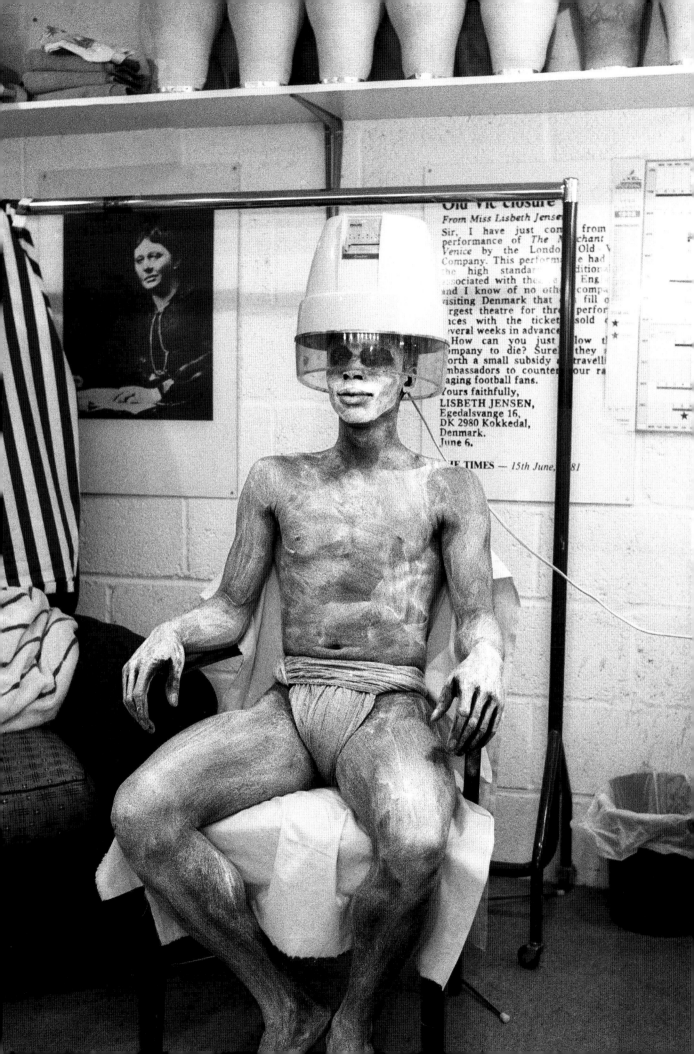

Old Vic closure

From Miss Lisbeth Jensen

Sir, I have just com__ from __
performance of *The M__chant*
Venice by the Londo__ Old V__
Company. This performa__e had
__e high standar__ __ditiona__
__ssociated with the__ a__ Eng__
__nd I know of no othe__ compa__
__isiting Denmark that __ fill o__
__rgest theatre for thre__ perfor__
__ces with the ticket__ sold o__
__veral weeks in advance__
__How can you just __llow th__
__ompany to die? Surel__ they __
__orth a small subsidy a__ travell__
__mbassadors to counter__our ra__
__aging football fans.
__ours faithfully,
LISBETH JENSEN,
Egedalsvange 16,
DK 2980 Kokkedal,
Denmark.
June 6.

__HE TIMES — 15th June, __81

PEGGY ASHCROFT as QUEEN KATHARINE
'KING HENRY THE EIGHTH'
(STRATFORD 1969)

232 **Tom Hardy**
Festen by David Eldridge, based on the film
and play by Thomas Vinterberg, Mogens Rukov
& Bo hr. Hansen
Almeida Theatre, 2004

Charlotte Emmerson
Baby Doll by Tennessee Williams
National Theatre, 1993

Lisa Dillon
Period of Adjustment by Tennessee Williams
Almeida Theatre, 2006

Rudolph Walker
Where There Is Darkness by Caryl Phillips
Lyric Theatre, Hammersmith, 1982

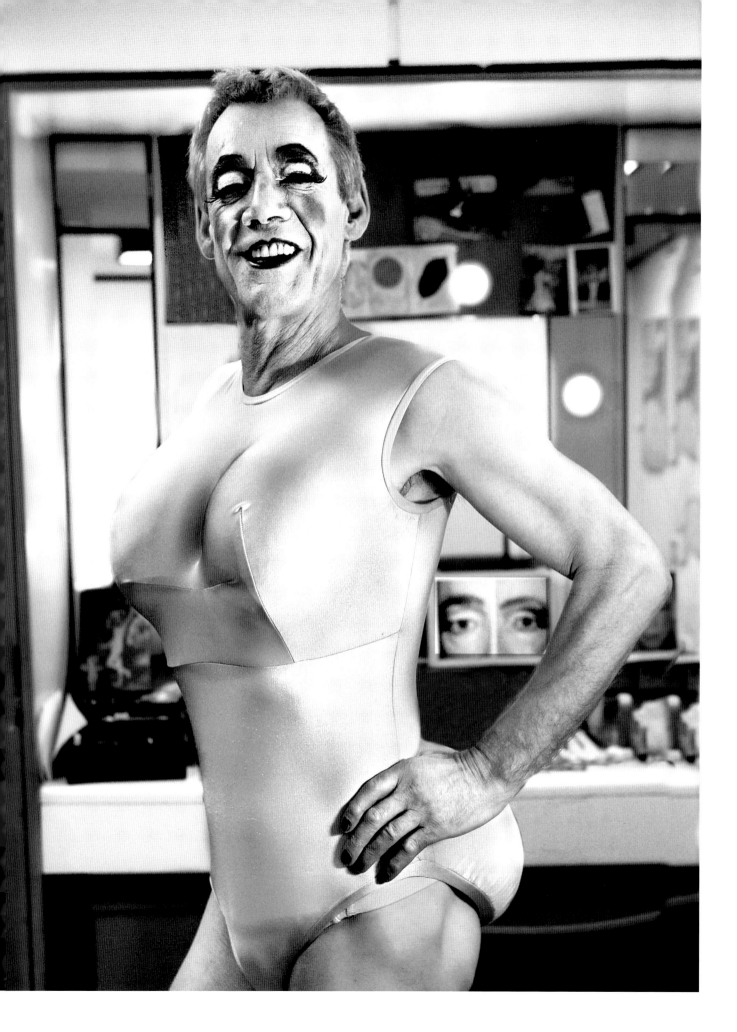

Roger Lloyd Pack
Dick Whittington by Mark Ravenhill
Barbican Theatre, 2006

Richard Wilson
Cinderella by Paul Hendy
New Wimbledon Theatre, 2005

Galina Panova
On Your Toes by Richard Rodgers,
Lorenz Hart & George Abbott
Palace Theatre, 1984

Linda Marlowe
Too Clever by Half by Alexander Ostrovsky,
adapted by Rodney Ackland
Old Vic Theatre, 1988

Alan Cumming
La Bête by David Hirson
Lyric Theatre, Hammersmith, 1992
About to make his entrance and crash
the cymbals

Tamzin Griffin
Shockheaded Peter by Julian Bleach, Anthony
Cairns, Julian Crouch, Graeme Gilmour, Tamzin
Griffin, Jo Pocock, Phelim McDermott, Michael
Morris & The Tiger Lillies
Piccadilly Theatre, 2001
Psyching herself up; props to her left, audience
behind the curtain to her right

From front, anticlockwise: **Rebecca Grant,
Alex Kingston, Lizzie Roper, Katherine
Jakeways, Owen O'Neill & Ian Coppinger**
One Flew Over the Cuckoo's Nest by Ken Kesey,
adapted by Dale Wasserman
Gielgud Theatre, 2004
An inmate prepares the nurses for the next scene

242 **Rudi Davies**
The Tempest by William Shakespeare
Old Vic Theatre, 1988

Juliette Lewis
Fool for Love by Sam Shepard
Apollo Theatre, 2006

Daniela Nardini
Camille by Alexandre Dumas,
adapted by Neil Bartlett
Lyric Theatre, Hammersmith, 2003

Michael Sheen
Look Back in Anger by John Osborne
National Theatre, 1999

Feeling below par with less than thirty
minutes before curtain-up

Richard Briers
Why Me? by Stanley Price
Strand Theatre, 1985

Paul Eddington
Jumpers by Tom Stoppard
Aldwych Theatre, 1984

Katrin Cartlidge
Mnemonic by Complicite
Riverside Studios, 2003

Emily Watson
Uncle Vanya by Anton Chekhov,
in a version by Brian Friel
Donmar Warehouse, 2002

Lynn Farleigh
The Skin Game by John Galsworthy
Orange Tree Theatre, 2007
Holding flowers she brought in
on the day a dear friend died

Judi Dench
The Royal Family by George S. Kaufman
& Edna Ferber
Theatre Royal Haymarket, 2002

Michael Williams
Two For One by Ray Cooney
Shaftesbury Theatre, 1984
A photo of his wife, Judi Dench, on
their wedding day is leaning against
the mirror

Colin Blakely
One for the Road by Harold Pinter
Theatre Royal, Bath, 1984

Donal McCann
The Steward of Christendom by Sebastian Barry
Royal Court Theatre, 1995

254 **Barbara Brennan**
By the Bog of Cats by Marina Carr
Wyndham's Theatre, 2004

Nabil Shaban
The Emperor by Ryszard Kapúscinki,
adapted by Jonathan Miller with Michael Hastings
Royal Court Theatre, 1987

Clive Francis
The Skin Game by John Galsworthy
Orange Tree Theatre, 2007

Emma Fielding
Private Lives by Noël Coward
Albery Theatre, 2001

Sophie Okonedo
The Vagina Monologues by Eve Ensler
New Ambassadors Theatre, 2001

Novella Nelson & Gugu Mbatha-Raw
Big White Fog by Theodore Ward
Almeida Theatre, 2007

Winston Ntshona & John Kani
Sizwe Banzi Is Dead
by Athol Fugard, John Kani & Winston Ntshona
National Theatre, 2007

Chiwetel Ejiofor
The Vortex by Noël Coward
Donmar Warehouse, 2002

Charles Dance
Good by C. P. Taylor
Donmar Warehouse, 1999

Anthony Hopkins
Pravda by Howard Brenton & David Hare
National Theatre, 1986

264   **Eric Porter**
King Lear by William Shakespeare
Old Vic Theatre, 1987

Glenn Close
A Streetcar Named Desire by Tennessee Williams
National Theatre, 2002

Kenneth Branagh
Public Enemy by Kenneth Branagh
Lyric Theatre, Hammersmith, 1987
Playing the lead in the Renaissance
Theatre Company's debut production

Kevin Spacey
Richard II by William Shakespeare
Old Vic Theatre, 2005

Josette Simon
The Vagina Monologues by Eve Ensler
New Ambassadors Theatre, 2001

Adrian Lester
Henry V by William Shakespeare
National Theatre, 2003

Tim Roth
Metamorphosis by Steven Berkoff
Mermaid Theatre, 1986

Gary Oldman
Serious Money by Caryl Churchill
Royal Court Theatre, 1987

Just before both actors started their
film careers in America

Brenda Blethyn
Benefactors by Michael Frayn
Vaudeville Theatre, 1984

Juliet Stevenson
Yerma by Federico García Lorca,
in a translation by Peter Luke
National Theatre, 1987

Michael Gambon
Old Times by Harold Pinter
Theatre Royal Haymarket, 1985

No cards or adornments. Joan Plowright
is pictured in the same room the
previous year for *The Way of the World*

Joss Ackland
Peter Pan by J. M. Barrie, adapted by
Carolyn Leigh & Mark Charlap
Aldwych Theatre, 1985
Playing both Mr Darling and Captain Hook

Zoë Wanamaker
Mother Courage and Her Children
by Bertolt Brecht, in a version by Hanif Kureishi
Barbican Theatre, 1984

Jane Asher
Henceforward by Alan Ayckbourn
Vaudeville Theatre, 1987

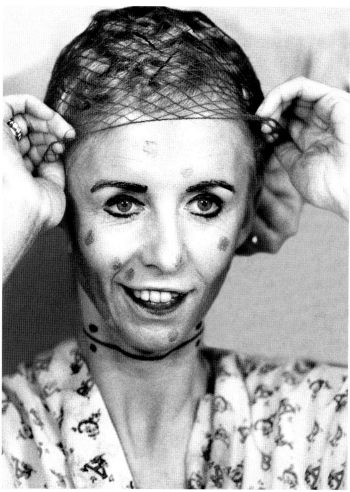

Joanne Whalley
Three Sisters by Anton Chekhov,
in a translation by Mike Alfreds
Greenwich Theatre, 1986

Julian Glover
Richard II by William Shakespeare
Old Vic Theatre, 2005

Derek Jacobi
The Tempest by William Shakespeare
Old Vic Theatre, 2003

Michael Maloney
Mouth to Mouth by Kevin Elyot
Royal Court Theatre, 2001

282

Anthony Andrews
The Letter by Somerset Maugham
Wyndham's Theatre, 2007
Just before he leaves his room for the
eight o'clock show

Christian Slater
One Flew over the Cuckoo's Nest
by Ken Kesey, adapted by Dale Wasserman
Gielgud Theatre, 2004
Pausing before he goes on

Emily Mortimer
The Lights by Howard Korder
Royal Court Theatre, 1996
On the fire escape

Matthew Modine
Resurrection Blues by Arthur Miller
Old Vic Theatre, 2006
Climbing stairs to the stage

Sally Leonard
A Family Affair by Alexander Ostrovsky,
in a translation by Nick Dear
Arcola Theatre, 2006
Waiting to go on. The audience can just be
seen in the background, taking their seats

Daniel Evans
The Tempest by William Shakespeare
Old Vic Theatre, 2002

Stephen Fry
The Common Pursuit by Simon Gray
Phoenix Theatre, 1988

Roger Sloman
The Mandate by Nikolai Erdman,
in a version by Declan Donnellan
National Theatre, 2004

Richard E. Grant
Otherwise Engaged by Simon Gray
Criterion Theatre, 2005

Simon Russell Beale
Hamlet by William Shakespeare
National Theatre, 2000
Looking across the
NT's famous courtyard

**Marcello Magni, Simon McBurney & Jos Houben
with company stage manager Cath Binks**
A Minute Too Late by Complicite
National Theatre, 2005
Standing in the dock off-stage, just before the show

**Fen Belling, Wendy Somerville, Neil Toon, Dermot
Canavan, Paul Manuel, Rachael Wooding, Leanne
Jones, Elinor Collett, Adrian Hansel, Michael Ball,
Zara Warren & Terel Nugent**
Hairspray by Brandon Thomas
Shaftesbury Theatre, 2008

Nicky Griffiths, Jenii Hicks, Tracie Bennett,
Rachael Wooding, Michael Ball & Leanne Jones
Hairspray by Brandon Thomas
Shaftesbury Theatre, 2008

Gina McKee
The Exonerated by Jessica Blank & Eric Jensen
Riverside Studios, 2007

Julian Bleach
Shockheaded Peter by Julian Bleach, Anthony
Cairns, Julian Crouch, Graeme Gilmour, Tamzin
Griffin, Jo Pocock, Phelim McDermott, Michael
Morris & The Tiger Lillies
Piccadilly Theatre, 2001

Eva Griffith
Terence Alexander
Charley's Aunt by Brandon Thomas
Lyric Theatre, Hammersmith, 1982
Two of the earliest pictures in this collection

Paterson Joseph
The Emperor Jones by Eugene O'Neill
Gate Theatre, London, 2005
Lying beneath the stage for ten minutes

302   *War Horse*, based on a novel by Michael Morpurgo,
adapted by Nick Stafford
National Theatre, 2008
Members of the company make their entrance
through the blacks onto the stage, leading the
horse, Joey, into battle

Olivia Williams, Clifford Samuel & Tom Hiddleston
The Changeling by Thomas Middleton & William Rowley
Barbican Theatre, 2006
Coming off stage, covered in blood

LIST OF ACTORS

Back in
5 mins

DOOR